STEPPING

from the

SHADOWS

EDWIN HOFERT

Balboa Press books may be ordered through booksellers or by contacting:

Balboa Press
A Division of Hay House
1663 Liberty Drive
Bloomington, IN 47403
www.balboapress.com
1 (877) 407-4847

ISBN: 978-1-4525-9573-3 (sc)
ISBN: 978-1-4525-9574-0 (e)

Printed in the United States of America.

Balboa Press rev. date: 05/30/2014

BALBOA.
PRESS
A DIVISION OF HAY HOUSE

Let me begin by saying that there has never been nor will there ever be. A poem written by me that in some way is not inspired by and dedicated to my dear mother. For without her there would be no me.

Dedication

I would like to dedicate Stepping From The Shadows to my daughter Jessica. Who loved me in spite of me. Who forgave me when others could not. And who cheers me on in nearly every attempt at anything new I've ever done. And to her husband Justin who is absolutely handpicked for her by God himself. And Their children. My grandchildren. Joey and Jacklyn who though time distance and circumstances prevented me from being there as much as I should have been. There has not been a breath taken by me since their births that they were not in my heart and on my mind.

Stepping from the shadows is my follow up book from Heart Whisperer. A collection of love poems.

And while there are still love poems in this second book there is a wide variety of others as well. It is divided into categories that at times seem to me to overlap. Thus is the nature of the poem.

While not every poem is for everyone. There is without a doubt something in almost every poem for each of us. A different message for all hidden among the stanzas that jog a memory back to life from long long ago. Some bring tears of joy while other bring smiles and laughter. While some the circumstances that led to their being written will never quite be fully understood as is true with the tribute section featuring poems written for Sandy Hook Elemtary. And the Boston Marathon runners.

Stepping From the Shadows is I believe the only name there could be for this my second book. And if I were to list all of the reasons why, it would be another book in and of itself. But I can give you a few good reasons before we venture off into the world of poetry.

After some life changing events in my own life I have spent the better part of the last three years locked away from almost everyone. No I was not in prison. At least not of steel and stone. Mine was made of flesh and bone. It was just me.

I had somehow imploded to the point I at times had very little desire to even live. Even though there were and still are many things in my life to be grateful for. I stayed in my darkened room sometimes for weeks without even turning on the TV for noise.

And then I began to write. It was far from the first time but this time it was different. One cold Jan morning about 3:00 am I tossed and turned and could not sleep. So I returned to my keyboard and computer where I had been spending all my days. And I began to write. And as I did things began to flow from the recesses of my heart and mind long ago forgotten even by me.

I felt myself and my poetry turn a corner.

That combined with a few caring pushes from a dear friend named Cindy Lewis and Heart Whisperer was born.

And that was the beginning of a runaway train.

I was Stepping from The shadows and I invite you to join me on my journey.

Welcome my friend.

Whoo Whoo! All Aboard!

The Wait

For so long in the shadows
I've been here all alone.
But I sense the time has come
to change my comfort zone.
Reaching out to others
no different than me;
Inviting them into the light
to see just what might be.

Waiting to be discovered
out here in the light.
Trying to be careful
while our eyes adjust from night.
Feeling with our hearts
our eyes closed from the sun,
Not returning to the shadows
until our days are done.

I was not kept hidden
Out of fear or even hate.
Something deep inside of me
Simply whispered, "Wait."
Now it seems my wait is over;
My turn now to shine.
Telling others just like me
It will all work out fine.

So step out of the shadows.
Come stand by my side.
There's a new train coming.
We don't want to miss this ride.
Answers to the questions
We've all asked before
Are waiting for us, every one,
Just beyond our door.

Edwin C Hofert

Contents

Dedication iv

The Wait... v

Yet To Find... 1

Hang On.. 2

Along Comes One!................................ 3

Picture In My Mind 3

When I Think of You 4

One You Gave To Me 5

Living Dreams. 5

The Moment... 6

Hope. 7

Brand New Move 8

Heart and Mind.................................... 9

Someday Man 10

Collide.. 11

The Seed 11

Silencing the Moon 12

The Brook.. 12

The Flower... 13

The Water.. 13

Falling Star. 14

Jaylens Tree 15

The Walk.. 15

Sea Of Tears... 16

Frozen for a Time 17

Most Important Moment...................... 18

Fear... 18

Didn't Matter Anyway.......................... 19

Chains 19

Land Of Living Dreams 20

The Angel On My Right 21

The Soul I Sold 21

Before Today is Done........................... 22

Rock Of Ages 22

Choices... 23

Let It Be 24

Death Is A Teacher 24

Bigger Than Me 25

Boston. 25

Oklahoma 26

A Cop... 27

Teacher Teacher 28

The Hero 28

You are One.. 29

Day Care 29

Step Mother 30

Prayer of Serenity 30

Crops in the Field 31

The Kind of Nurse that You Could
Be 31

Two Sisters 32

Give It All To Him 33

Grace 34

The Potter.. 34

Written In Red 35

For Granted.. 35

Empty Tomb 36

He Holds Tomorrow 37

Parables and Poetry............................. 37

The Sparrow 38

Judgment over me................................ 38

Give It All To Me 39

Jesus Had Been Here. 40

Gravy Train.. 41

The Only One I Missed!....................... 42

The Cleaner 42

Desire 43

Full Grown Girl................................... 44

Digging all of you. 44

Holiday Romance!................................ 45

Cereal Killer... 45

Call Out My Name. 46

Well-Mart... 47

Rise Again 48

Suddenly... 48

Unbroken.. 49

The Longing: A Mothers Love 50

Let Her Go. 50

"My Only One" 51

One More Before I Go 51

Going Home. 52

Angels Wing. 53

Dearly Beloved 54

Hide Out In The Open. 56

Depressions Confessions 57

Aaron 57

Sleeping With The Enemy 58

The climb 59

My World That I Call Chase 59

The Battle Rages.................................. 60

His Fix 60

Playground In My Mind.................. 61

Yet To Find

Should tomorrow you awaken
and I've left this world behind.
Will you think of all the wonders
that I have yet to find?

Or will you be filled with sorrow
for things we didn't say?
The times we missed each other
cause life got in the way.

Will you celebrate the time we had
all the things we shared?
Or be filled with regret
not saying that you cared?

Will you recall the good times

and all the laughs we had?
Or cling to things that we can't change
that make your heart feel bad?

The only thing that's different
than it was from the start.
I'm no longer by your side
I'm living in your heart.

So turn toward the heavens
dry tears from your eyes.
Show the smile I long to see
as I look from the skies.

Edwin C Hofert

HANG ON.

During the struggles we all face, each of us every one.
Night is always darkest just before the night is done.
We tell ourselves just hang on. Hang on for one more day.
Soon enough we will see our troubles slip away.

Yet some of them still linger. Like scars no one can see.
If I were there with you now I'd get down on one knee.
I would look deeply in your eyes and then try to explain.
That all my words of light and love were at one time words of pain.

You have worked a miracle in the man before you now.
That it was God that chose you to be the one somehow.
You unlocked all the secrets and to set my spirit free.
I may never have the words to say. What you mean to me.

But as I knelt down before you I would take your hand.
And beg you to forgive me for things I don't understand.
How we've touched each other, how you help me cope.
The way you inspired me. You've given me some hope.

If you see a glimpse of ghosts that made me who I am.
It's because I trust in you. And believe you give a damn.
I ask you to hang on with me. Hang on for one more day.
And if you must hang on to me and don't let me slip away.

Along Comes One!

Thank you for the times you heard exactly what I said.
And for knowing that what I meant was exactly what you read

And thank you for responding each time that you did.
Instead of trying to search for some meaning that I hid.

Sometimes when I consider the cards we all get dealt.
I wonder if I'm wasting time if my words are ever felt.

And then somehow along comes one like a shot out of the blue.
Bringing with them a special gift and dear. That one is you.

A gift that's called perception a rare gift it is indeed.
I wonder how it is you knew that I was so in need.

I guess what matters most to me, is not to have you on some list.
The thing that matters most to me is just knowing you exist.

Like rain is to a flower, that's drowning in the sun.
Everybody may be different yet everybody needs someone.

You came when I needed you most it's like you were heaven sent.
The only one that read my words and felt just what I meant.

There are those that claim to see straight
through the words I write.
But only you can feel them in the middle of the night.

Picture In My Mind

The first time I laid eyes on you.
I'd seen you before.
Still my heart cried out.
My eyes longed for more.

I looked at your picture.
As my heart longed to see,
If somewhere in your picture.
There might be room for me.

I studied every move.
I imagined you would make.
I wanted to be near you.
A new picture we could take.

One of just your hands.
Being held in mine.
In the background just your eyes.
And the way they shine.

A picture in a picture.
My hands on your hips.
As I hold you close to me.
My lips on your lips.

If you look inside me.
The picture you will find.
Where I've seen you so many times.
The picture in my mind

When I Think of You

Have you wanted one so badly? That it changed how you live?
That as you looked around you there's nothing you wouldn't give.

To have them in your presence to be yours to have and hold.
To keep them there close with you when the nights grow cold.

To see their smile as it forms and spreads across their face.
The missing piece of your life that puts everything in place.

To wake up in the morning glad that you're alive.
Wondering without them how did you survive?

To see the light in their eyes you know, you don't assume.
When their looking at you as you walk into the room.

A desire that runs so deep it goes from want to need.
Like faith that moves the mountains that started as a seed.

These are the ways I feel in everything I do.
It is my motivation when I think of you.

One You Gave To Me

From the first time that I saw you. I knew you were unique.
But nothing could prepare me. For when I heard you speak.

It was like the sunshine. Suddenly had a voice.
All I could do was smile. As if I had no choice.

It sounded like a symphony. You were music in my ear.
I closed my eyes to pretend. That you were standing here.

We talked for quite awhile. I treasured every minute.
As I thought how much better. My life is with you in it.

I enjoyed your giggles. I just love your spirit.
I will always hope and pray. To someday just be near it.

I've been thinking since then. For a way to show to you.
How much I admire. Everything you do.

So when your sky is cloudy. And your sun can't seem to shine.
If you have trouble smiling. I'll send you one of mine.

Much like paying forward. By helping you to see.
That every smile I give you. Is one you gave to me.

Living Dreams.

I know everybody dreams, they don't always come true.
Still somehow I find comfort in the dreams I dream of you.

There may be no room for me in all the dreams you've made.
But darling even if that's true I not only dreamed I prayed.

My dreams could be kept secret but how I show I care.
It's in the dreams and other things that I choose to share.

So if my dream is not yours you don't feel it in your heart.
It's just a silly dream I dream whenever we're apart.

The secret of all dreams and what makes dreams come true.
A dream can't live with just one heart a living dream takes two.

When two people dream together or
when they dream the same.
They send life to one another in that there is no shame.

But a dream left alone to live no matter how it might try.
Without that second beating heart
that dream someday will die.

So let me dream while I'm alive all the dreams that I want to.
Lest the dreams I dream will die if not for dreams of you.

The Moment

A picture paints a thousand words. To me yours says much more.
Your smile seems to draw me in. Your eyes I now adore.

It speaks to me of wanting. Like the way I want you now.
It calls me to reach out to you. I confess I don't know how.

Words come a mile a minute. As I look at you this way.
But when it comes down to it I'm filled with doubt for what to say.

The things that are heavy on my heart. I fear I must not admit.
Like I think about you constantly and I'm powerless to quit.

When it comes to my thoughts of you I'm as helpless as a child.
All I know is what I want, my imagination's running wild.

I continue to live my life. As I'm sure that you do yours.
I've burnt so many bridges and closed behind me many doors.

Suddenly I'm not so eager to move past this time and place.
Inside me lives a hunger to gently touch your face.

To let that moment take us. Wherever we are to go.
It pains me just to think about. What we may never know.

I'll think of you tomorrow. Just like all day today.
Holding you in my heart and mind until I find a way.

Hope.

The most exciting frightening feeling many will ever know.
Will be when true love finds them and they feel it start to grow.

It seems to start when sleep at night is suddenly hard to find.
You try but can't deny love is on your mind.

Then in some conversation you realize that it's true.
Love has found a secret path and now it's in there too.

You silently consider what you once hid to cope.
The love you ran away from is like hoping against hope.

The fear that once held you at bay now seems unjustified.
You wonder at what you told yourself could it be you lied?

When you said you weren't lonely when you said you weren't blue.
Is it even possible you were only fooling you.

The walls you built around your heart suddenly start to crack.
You know where it's leading and there's no turning back.

Then without a word of warning you're no longer in a storm.
A peace begins to fall on you. Now you feel safe and warm.

You can run and you can hide from all things up above.
But there's no use in hiding when you know you are in love.

Brand New Move

You say your heart is tethered? Mine is tethered too.
The biggest difference is, mine is locked on you.

It's not about right or wrong or just and unjust.
It's not about my thoughts of you being thoughts of lust.

It's just that looking at your smile is my favorite thing to do.
Life to me is better just knowing I know you.

So I write words of adoration and words of sweet romance.
Knowing all the while that this is how we dance.

As I write my poetry with every verse or two.
I'm walking cross the dance floor to make my way to you.

As you read my words of praise I'm trying to catch your eye.
Your response is how I know if I should or should not try.

When you answer with a smile I take you by the hand.
Then I ask for the next dance hoping that you stand.

While we're chatting back and forth that's when I find my groove.
Next thing that you know we're busting a brand new move.

Heart and Mind

I saw the picture of you. By my heart my mind was led.
It seemed to stir a conflict between my heart and head.

There was not a contest as to the beauty that I see.
My heart tried to convince my mind that you were meant for me.

My mind quickly countered that you have another love.
That you are joined together, in the eyes of God above.

My heart kept beating faster than it ever has before.
And it kept trying to reason with my mind some more.

So they asked my eyes to be the final judge.
My eyes read you're taken but my heart would not budge.

So we sat down together but I knew right from the start.
Before this day was over I'd be torn apart.

And so it was decided. I knew what I must do.
I must turn and walk away. And leave my heart with you.

Someday Man

Sometimes late at night they'd talk camping out by the stream.
They would talk til the sun came up as she listened to him dream.

He'd say someday they would see the world. Someday he'd be a star.
Someday he would start a band. Someday he'd go far.

She watched his eyes as he talked. She heard every word he'd say.
But she knew as she listened. He'd never even learn to play.

He talked about life together. All the things they'd see and do.
And she would smile and hold his hand. Not all dreams come true.

She loved to hear his stories while he told her of his plan.
He was and would always be her lovin someday man.

He told of all the things in store their future was looking bright.
She hoped someday he'd never know sometimes she cried at night.

With far too many bills to pay, and so little coming in.
She worked two jobs all week long but she loved him even then.

Someday he would buy her. A great big diamond ring
Someday he would promise her he'd give her everything.

But she loved him in spite of him and she did ever thing she can.
As she stood right beside him her lovin someday man.

Collide

The heavens fill with beauty.
It comes as no surprise.
No matter if the sun sets.
Or if it's time to rise.

It happens every night.
Where angels all abide.
Then again each morning.
When day and night collide.

The colors are beyond words.
And yet they tell the story.
Up there in the heavens.
Of God and all His glory.

They serve as a reminder.
Of everything that's good.
Helping us appreciate.
All the things we should.

A moment of reflection.
As we look up at the skies.
Helping us to notice.
The look in a lovers eyes.

Giving us a sample.
Of God and all His pride.
Asking only that we think of Him.
When day and night collide.

The Seed

I hear groaning in the distance an aching crashing sound.
The noise a mighty oak makes. As it lay's on the ground.

After years of service, providing shade for all.
Many never knowing someday that tree might fall.

The memories bestowed on it will all be left behind.
Because you can't lose a picture, that's etched upon your mind.

A heart carved in its bark with a lover's name.
Though the tree has fallen their love remains the same.

Memories of the branches, reaching high into the skies.
The leaves providing shelter from sun shine in your eyes.

Fallen branches fueled the fires when there was a need.
This mighty oak that's fallen was once a tiny seed.

The storms that it has weathered the secrets it has kept.
Giving home to the birds where their babies slept.

Gone but not forgotten memories abound.
The big oak has not fallen it's just lying down.

Silencing the Moon

Everything in creation
speaks to the heart of man.
Like waves pounding from the ocean
against the rocks and sand.

Raindrops on an old tin roof
thunder rolling in the skies.
The way a lover speaks to you
using nothing but their eyes.

The wind that softly touches you
as it slows to just a breeze.
The way the forest dances
as it blows through the trees.

The stirring deep inside of you
when you see a star fall.
A rainbow in the distance
as it speaks to us all.

A church bell in a steeple
though seldom does it ring.
Finds a way to speak to us
though it never say's a thing.

As we look around the world
we find understanding soon.
That quieting all creation
is like silencing the moon.

The Brook

Walking through the wilderness, that is or was my soul.
Fearing I might die from thirst. Not finding a watering hole.
I searched both far and wide. There was no place else to look.
I was just about to give up when I happened upon a brook.
It was a thing of beauty unlike anything I'd seen.
Its water ran so clear and deep its grass and trees so green.

There were birds and butterflies each singing their own song.
And I began to wonder where life had gone so wrong.
I found my way beside the brook. I bent down to take a drink.
When I looked into the water I could not speak or think.
My reflection showed me young again! My face was shaven clean!
I drew back from the water! Asking what does all this mean?

I ran my fingers through my beard. Then I touched my face.
I realized almost at once I found my happy place.
I inched back toward the water then I slowly peeked inside.
I saw me laughing as a child as then I ran to hide.
I saw every memory that had made my life worth living.
Filled with joy and happiness tenderness and forgiving.

I put my face into the water and drank deeply from the brook.
And then sat down in the grass and laughed so hard I shook.
When the laughter all subsided it was such a sweet release.
I quietly looked around my soul that now was filled with peace.
I looked back into the water my old face had returned.
While peaceful still, memories of bridges I had burned.

I stood looking at the water then I began to see.
That somehow when I found this brook I stumbled upon me.

The Water

Out here by the water
the skies are all so blue.
As I treasure every second
that I'm out here with you.

The sound of laughter echoes
and goes straight to my heart.
I wonder how I made it
through all the years apart.

Birds all singing love songs
as the water rushes by.
Even without wings
I feel like I could fly.

How can it be that heaven
could be this very place?
I swear I see an angel
when I look at your face.

It seems almost like walking
on top of a cloud.
Should life be this good
is this all allowed.

Could it be a reflection?
Am I blinded by the sun?
Will I ever be the same?
When this day is done?

Surrounded by this beauty
it comes as no surprise.
I am overwhelmed
by the light that's in your eyes.

The Flower

Today I saw a flower I knew just what to do.
Pluck it from its hiding spot and bring it back to you.
As I bent down to grab it, from its resting place.
I saw past the smile this flower would bring your face.
I looked inside your heart. And saw the gift that I must give
I stood and slowly walked away. And let the flower live.

FALLING STAR.

The stars hold their position in the sky above.
Keeping track of wishes from those below in love.
The moon watches closely the mother of them all.
Deciding which of all the stars will be the next to fall.

The sun has his part to do watching from far away.
Seeing lovers loving, throughout the light of day.
He sends a message to the moon when he knows the time is right.
He tells her to be ready tomorrow night's the night.

The moon picks out the chosen one they set the time and date.
Then all of heaven grows excited as they all watch and wait.
Down below the lovers walking down an unlit street.
Or holding hands along a shore where lovers often meet.

Though many different couples are miles and miles apart.
As the star begins its fall they all share one lovers heart.
Then only for a second just the twinkling of an eye.
As the lovers wish upon the star time freezes in the sky.

The heavens all grow silent so the moon and stars won't miss.
The magic of the moment hidden in their lovers kiss.
So? You ask what happened? To the star that fell?
I really shouldn't say this. I promised not to tell.

But the falling star never fell. It was his debut.
He gathers up and carries back. The wishes from me and you.

Jaylens Tree

Planted as a sapling
it grew so big and tall.
Providing years of service
as well as shade for all.

High up in its branches
a place where birds abide.
A little farther down
where Jaylen used to hide.

A grand silver maple
grew bigger than you planned.
Its leaves served as the padding
where Jaylen used to land.

As he jumped from the branches
where little boys would play.
No one ever thinking
it might be gone some day.

Time goes by so fast these days
it seems almost insane.
But memories of Jaylens tree
forever will remain.

The Walk

If you could look into my eyes I know what you would see.
You would see my very heart looking out at you from me.
From a distance I'm no different than anyone else you know.
But if you were to come closer there is much more here to show.
We could chat for hours on end or call on the phone and talk.
But if you could step inside me I'd take you for a walk.
You see those mountains over there I've climbed them all but one.
But I still hope to master it before my life is done.

Up there in the rocks you see the bones of dragons I have slain.
I fought with everything I had until not one of them remain.
Along this muddy river are the shells of bridges I have burned.
Inside this old tattered book are the lessons I have learned.
This river we are standing near that looks so deep and wide.
It's not made of rain from heaven it's made from tears I cried.
The mansion on that hill right there on its door you'll find my name.
No one lives there anymore that's my house of shame.

On down this road a little ways will put a smile on your face.
Because right around the corner you'll see my happy place.
It's filled with all the things I've done that made somebody smile.
If you start getting tired we could rest here for awhile.
Though there's more much more to see you're welcome anytime.
We can come back later perhaps some other rhyme.
You see that bright light shining we're not quite finished yet.
That light's the smile you gave me the first moment that we met.

It helps me weather every storm with wind and rain unfurled.
So what your smile does for me is it lights up my whole world.

Sea Of Tears

I saw her in the distance, she looked so all alone.
I asked what's a girl like you doing out here on your own?

She said she comes here sometimes, when life gets to be too much.
This was the very last place she felt her mother's touch.

We sat quiet for a moment. I began to silently pray.
That God would give me guidance, as well as words to say.

I looked out to the ocean as we stood there on the beach.
And thanked God up in heaven, there is none He cannot reach.

Then I told her the story of how the ocean got its start.
It all began with a girl like her. That once had a broken heart.

This young girl cried day and night. She even cried in her dreams.
But God saves every single tear. So He created streams.

Still she cried and cried and cried, no comfort one could give her.
Then God began to channel streams so they would feed the river.

The river finally found its way to where it's been all these years.
That girl was your mother. That cried this sea of tears.

Wishing only happiness and that all your dreams come true.
That you would know wherever you go that she is there with you.

She's in the breeze that comforts you. You will never be apart.
Your mother has not gone away. She lives inside your heart.

Frozen for a Time

A tree is strongest. When it's strong enough to bend.
As it stands the test of time .Braced against the wind.

There are many lessons. In this life that we must learn.
Like to cross a bridge or when that bridge must burn.

The storms of life come calling. You can't take no more.
But only wind and rain. Come beating down your door.

You feel you've lost your way. And you can't find a friend.
Days that even water. Is found bending in the wind.

If only for a moment. No reason and no rhyme.
Together past and present. Are frozen for a time.

Take a chance on this day. To reach out for tomorrow.
For the sun will shine again. And melt away your sorrow.

Most Important Moment.

Shining in the distance
the sun bids us goodnight.
No promise of returning
next morning at daylight.

So smile while you're able
share laughter if you can.
Hug you're lover closely
hold somebody's hand.

Reach deeply inside you
and let your feelings show.
Lest darkness come upon you
then they may never know.

All those that bring you joy
just having them so near.
The words you long to share
the words they long to hear.

Tomorrows not a promise
no matter what your plans.
A wise man listens with his heart
then he understands.

The most important moment
the best thing you can give.
The one thing within your reach
the next moment that you live.

FEAR

There might be trouble waiting right on down the lane.
There might be some heartache or some other pain.
Should we live in fear? Of what may or may not come?
Or do we stand in faith until our days are done?

Do we stand with courage? Put faith in God above?
Or should we run and hide? From matters such as love?
My hearts been broken often .and it might break more.
But you can bet I'll open it if you knock upon my door.

Fear is like a cloud of fog. When you're in it looks dense.
But if you rise above the fog it's not nearly as intense.
If you give fear a stronghold. Then no matter what you do.
You can't let go of something. That's holding onto you.

So break the chains that bind you. Set your spirit free.
It's the way you'll find out. If something's meant to be.
Go for what you're wanting taking one step at a time.
Don't let fear convince you. That loving is a crime.

Didn't Matter Anyway.

It's hard to find a reason.
Or even words to say.
When you suddenly realize
you didn't matter anyway.

You try to hide the pain.
But your tears give you away.
No sense trying to explain it.
There are no words to say.

You did all you knew to do.
You did your very best.
Maybe the thing to do now
go home and get some rest.

Rest your wounded spirit.
And rest your wounded pride.
I stand with arms wide open
if you just step inside.

Time will heal your wounds I'm told
if you can wait that long.
Love can fix a broken heart.
Only love can make you strong.

Time is of the essence.
Time has its role to play.
After a little time you'll see.
They didn't matter anyway.

Chains

At times we fear the most. What we need fear the least.
Fear takes hold inside of us and becomes a raging beast.

Convincing us we must not try to think outside the box.
Making us all prisoners of fears chains and locks.

Making us believe at times our dreams cannot come true.
Building unseen walls around, both me and you.

Keeping us from reaching out settling for what we know.
Robbing us of courage fear's allowed to grow.

Take just one step today. Then tomorrow make it two.
Set your heart and mind on. What you know you must do.

Break the chains around you. Spread your wings and try.
Dreams don't wait forever. You first must learn to fly.

Land Of Living Dreams

In the land of living dreams, nothing cannot be done.
If you dream all alone or with your chosen one.

It's not that life is easy or never so demanding.
But the land of living dreams is filled with understanding.

You can walk or run real fast. Or give your wings a voice.
Everything you do here is always done by choice.

You can undo heartache if you concentrate.

There is only love here. No anger and no hate.

The birds all sing forever. There is no need for sleep.
There's no need for tears. No reason here to weep.

You can walk on the clouds. Reach out and touch the stars.
Travel where you want to without trucks or cars.

In the land of living dreams your dreams all come true.
Because in the land of living dreams. It all depends on you.

The Angel On My Right

Devil to the left of me an angel on my right.
The devil whispered quietly let's go out tonight.

Glancing at the angel she asked what'd he say?
You might say I lied. He asked the time of day.

He kept on insisting. He said it would be fun.
But I knew it would send my angel on the run.

Go on out without me have fun kick up your heels.
We'll stay here without you I know that's how the angel feels.

Looking all dejected he said I should tell her that you lied.
I did not ask the time and that you're evil deep inside.

I looked into my angels eyes before this became a mess.
I told her I was sorry and proceeded to confess.

The moral to this story, among many other things.
If you bargain with the devil don't be surprised he sings.

He uses one small victory to defeat you even more.
You're better off not letting him get into your minds door

The Soul I Sold

In the dream I dreamed last night.
The world was dark and cold.
I had returned back into hell.
To retrieve the soul I sold.

Surrounded by my enemies
not one friend did I see.
I tried to save another
the way that He saved me.

As I looked all around me
I heard the souls that cried.
My enemy stayed hidden.
From the light I had inside.

Finally I found my soul.
It was lost and all alone.
I laid hold upon it.
And I claimed it as my own.

Throughout my journey into hell
I was constantly under attack.
They could no longer hurt me.
And I did not fight back.

I found another lying there.
Her heart broke in two.
I reached out to hold her.
And I carried her out too.

Before Today is Done

In this life I lived and learned what it is that lasts.
Hopes and dreams and memories
and scars left from the past.

Hopes that weather every storm hope for a bright tomorrow.
Hope for joy and happiness and the end of all our sorrow.

Dreams that give us reason to see beyond today.
Dreams that just grow greater, than things left in the way.

Memories of love that's found and of love that's lost.
Memories of understanding what it is love cost.

The scars left by the victories and losses big and small.
Scars that help us rise again each and every time we fall.

Hope creates the dreams and some of them come true.
Then they become the memories that help to get us through.

The scars serve as reminders of just how far we've come.
Creating hope for tomorrow before today is even done.

Rock Of Ages

The story's told of two that came
to build upon the land.
One built his house on the rock
the other in the sand.

Both were homes of beauty
on the shore out by the sea.
People came from far and wide.
Just to look and see.

The skies became all cloudy.
The wind began to blow.
The people ran for shelter
as fast as they could go.

The rain beat down upon them.
At first they both stood firm.
Herein God found a lesson
for all mankind to learn.

The house that was built upon the rock
did not so much as shake.
The house built upon the sand.
The mighty storm did take.

So in making your foundation
make it strong and true.
Jesus Rock of Ages
will last the whole storm through.

As seen throughout all history.
A house just cannot stand.
If you choose your foundation
built upon the sand.

Choices

I can't shake this feeling. Disappointment or is it dread?
Is it aching in my heart? Or is it just in my head?

Is this how a flower feels? As it starves for lack of rain?
Or is it just the way it feels? When a heart finds it's in pain?

Will it go away again? Or is it here to stay?
Because if you were to ask me. I've always felt this way.

Early in the morning or even late at night.
I wake with this feeling .That something isn't right.

With my eyes wide open. And even in my dreams.
Surrounded by the silence I hear my hearts screams.

Crying out and longing. For more than I possess.
Is there more I can do? Something I must confess?

Strong I am in body. Though my spirits weak.
All I find are questions to answers that I seek.

From one day to another this journey that I make.
All depends on choices and the chances that I take.

LET IT BE

As they kept getting closer, you drew farther away.
Left with no one to turn to, all the colors turned to gray.
Skies have turned all cloudy I can't tell day and night apart.
The pain I feel from loving you is how I tell I have a heart.

I've given up believing, that anything will be ok.
And you've given up believing, in anything I say.
As far as my emotions, I can't feel anything at all.
I spend each minute hoping, that you will or will not call.

One minute I would give the world to have you by my side.
The next I want to run away, crawl in a hole and hide.
I miss your laughter, your smile and your touch.
I had no way of knowing, I could miss someone so much.

I could not change our future, now it's in the past.
Is it possible that heart ache, will be the part of us to last?
There are times I want another, mostly out of spite.
But it would be like using a wrong to make another right.

Each day that I make it through, is another battle fought.
Just like other mistakes I've made, another lesson taught.
I feel like the sole survivor, on a ship tossed around at sea.
But I've learned that if you can't fix it. You must learn to
"let it be"
Inspired by: A time of trials

Death Is A Teacher

(Sandy Hook Elementary)
The first Christmas without them
Our lives forever changed.
In just a matter of moments
Our lives are rearranged.

Too late now to fix it
The evil that's been done.
Hearts broken around the world
by a madman and his gun.

Just another day at school
then in a single breath.
A new teacher entered.
That teachers name was death.

Angels lined up at the school
to escort little ones to heaven.
And adults who gave their lives
except one from twenty seven.

Too early now to know for sure
what we're supposed to learn.
There are some that will never see
healing take its turn.

People asking where was God?
On that fateful day.
He had sent the angels.
To help the children find their way.

BIGGER THAN ME

(Hurricane Sandy)
To those on the east coast
filled with fear and doubt.
Feeling the brutality
of forces from without.

I offer what I have to you.
What I offer you is free.
Do not underestimate
the fact that I offer me.

To those on the east coast
whose heart is filled with pain.
I long to be there with you
to help after all the rain.

Help put things in order.
Turn things back around.
Clean up from the ocean.
That has washed aground.

Rebuild your home or business
vacuum out your car.
Rebuild your home churches.
Or fix up your local bar.

To be a part of something
much bigger than myself.
I just need a moment.
To get my tools down off the shelf.

BOSTON.

(Boston marathon bombings)

To those injured in Boston out running for a cause.
What you are enduring has made the world to pause.

As we stand in the distance. Though miles away from you.
Even while you suffer the whole world suffers too.

We have you on our hearts and in our prayers each day.
In that we stand beside you in the prayers we pray.

Saddened by the state we're in saddened by those lost.
United in our freedom yet saddened by its cost.

Though this very moment all you can say is "Why?"
We may never understand it no matter how we try.

The hate that others harbor though we've done no wrong.
In our lack of understanding together we are strong

In spite of all the tragedies and miles between you and I.
We remain as one. In freedom til we die.

Oklahoma

(Tornado of 2013)

Sometimes Lord there are no words we don't know what to say.
At times like this we turn to You asking Lord please help us pray.

You see beyond what we see we're so thankful that You care.
We thank You for being here Lord we thank You for being there.

With those in Oklahoma whose homes are torn apart.
As they work through the devastation give courage for their hearts.

For those that lost a loved one in the storm and wind and rain.
We ask you give them comfort please help them through their pain.

And as they struggle to perceive the tragedy the waste.
Please forgive those hurting that blame You in their haste.

As the whole world comes together to help them in their plight.
Lead them someplace warm and safe help them sleep at night.

Send to them your angels as they rebuild again.
Bless them where they need it show them how to begin.

Mostly Lord we thank You for protecting those You did.
Send them a reminder let not their faith be hid.

In Jesus name Amen.

A Cop

You rise to the occasion. For the oath you've taken.
To serve and to protect your integrity unshaken.

There's no suit of armor for all that you must do.
Yet you stand as one a brotherhood of blue.

So few people notice those tender moments shared.
When guided by your heart. You showed someone you cared.

The child that's going hungry and groceries that you bought.
How you live day by day. Giving all you've got.

The risk you take upon yourself by day and then by nights.

Each time you are prompted to use your flashing lights.

Wherever there is trouble. You go where you must.
Protecting those that are weak from those that are unjust.

You wear your badge with honor proudly on your breast.
Defined by the heart that beats inside your chest.

Considering all the good you do. Please don't ever stop.
The whole wide world is safer because you became a cop.

Teacher Teacher

Inspired by and dedicated to my dear
friend Penny Weatherly Duer

A teacher walks the hallway
filled with hope and grace.
The look of determination
is etched into her face.

She's not trying to save them all.
She won't settle for just one.
She wants them to save themselves.
Only then her job is done.

Until then her eyes are open
looking for that one lost child.
In hopes to inspire him
and keep him from running wild.

To build in him the confidence
that as a man he'll need.
To reach into his mind
and plant some fertile seed.

That it may grow within him.
Grow, multiply and abound.
So that he can then help others.
With the knowledge he has found.

Building on the future
high hopes for all mankind.
The answers this one found in her.
In him they too shall find.

It only takes one teacher
to inspire one boy or girl.
It only takes one teacher
to inspire the whole wide world.

The Hero

A tribute to our Firemen.

He's not really crazy. He has a hero's heart.
When people are in danger he wants to do his part.

So anytime a call comes in. He puts on all his gear.
And goes where he is needed be it far or near.

Once at his destination he surveys the scene.
When he yells to stand back he's not being mean.

He's trying to protect you to keep you from harm.
It's his call to duty. He's not here for the charm.

When he hears somebody scream trapped on the second floor.
Without a moment's hesitation he busts down the door.

He runs in the burning building when all others run away.
He pushes through smoke and flames vowing, no one dies today.

He finds them coughing, choking picks them up off the floor.
Carries them on his shoulder down the steps, and out the door.

He's not really crazy he has a fireman's heart
If he had it his way the fire would never start.

You are One

Caregiver Tribute

You get up every morning.
Make sure everyone is dressed.
You do it without thought.
But still you do your best.
You dish out medications.
You make sure they're okay.
And you do it all before
You even start your day.

Time to do some laundry.
There's the yard to mow.
Everybody is aware.
Yet you somehow don't know.
It's you that makes life worth living.
For those for whom you care.
They wouldn't last a week..
Without you being there.

You've done it for so long now.
You could not even cope.
If there weren't somebody else.
That you could give some hope.
You face the challenges as they come.
You take it all in stride.
But late at night when you're alone.
You feel the hurt inside.

Wishing it were different.
Wishing they were well.
Wishing you could save them all.
From their brush with hell.
The thought of what you know to be.
Causes you to shiver.
Time has come to face the truth.
You are their caregiver.

Day Care

When you rise up in the morning.
You prepare to face the day.
You can't wait to get started.
You love to watch them play.
Seldom ever thinking thoughts.
Like you wish to be alone.
You're surrounded by the little ones.
That you treat like your own.

There may be another day care.
But care is what you give.
Doing what you love to do.
This is the life you chose to live.
Helping them work through fears.
When they miss their mom and dad.
Giving out little hugs.
Should they start feeling bad.

Teaching them good values.
Such things like how to share.
All are things that you supply.
As you provide day care.
Helping them begin their life.
Right from the very start.
Praising them for being good.
God bless their little heart.

Seeing that they eat right.
Keeping track of what they drink.
Even reading little minds.
So that you know what they think.
Thinking all night long.
About when they are there.
That's the love they find.
In the arms of your day care.

Step Mother

Tribute

New into the family.
Often misunderstood.
What's taken for bad.
That you mean for good.
Complications from within.
When you're from without.
As you make a family.
When there's some that doubt.

A lack of understanding.
The gift sent from above.
Trying to find agendas.
When you're there for the love.
It seems that there is always.
One that looks for wrong.
Not knowing that all you're doing.
Is trying to stay strong.

For the love that you have found.
The one you stand beside.
He is the only reason.
That you became his bride.
But the love you found.
Is true and strong and pure.
Keep doing what you're doing.
Your love will endure.

For children of all ages.
Sometimes misunderstand.
The reason for the being.
A gold ring on your hand.
Not accepting of the future.
And your love for one another.
Still trying and denying.
You're now their step mother

Prayer of Serenity

Service men and women tribute

I come to You Lord Jesus.
I'm down on my knees.
I pray as I turn to You.
You will hear my plea's.

Care for sons and daughters.
That have gone off to war.
They defend our freedom.
And they do so much more.

They are brothers and sisters.
They are a mom and dad.
Please bring them home safely.
Don't let this thing end bad.

Care for all their families.
While they're so far away.
Until finally "Welcome Home"
They hear us proudly say.

Keep their children safe from harm.
Help them know that it's alright.
So their minds are not torn.
As they fight freedoms fight.

Send them loves reminders.
Of how much they are missed.
And bring them back to their own.
To be hugged and kissed.

To God be the Glory.
As we offer up this praise.
And may we strive to serve You.
Each one, all our days.

Crops in the Field

Farmers Tribute

He stands out by his tractor. He's worried about his yield.
It hasn't rained in a month. You could see it in his field.
He thinks about his family. Their dreams are his hope.
If he should lose his grandfather's farm how will they all cope.

Without a single glance around he got down on his knees.
He said Lord I'm sorry. Can't you help me please?
I know that I'm not perfect. I damn sure aint no saint.
Them crops sure need some water the
barn could use some paint.

I been doing right by you three Sundays in a row.
Each week I prayed for water. So my crops could grow.
My boy wants to go to college. But I've spent my last dime.
So here I am just me and You. I'm asking one last time.

His voice began to crack from the stress that he was under.
It scared him right up on his feet as the sky began to thunder.
He looked to his left and right his eyes filled with pride.
His wife and son and daughter were praying by his side.

If anyone had seen them all they'd swear they've gone insane.
Out there in that down pour dancing in the rain.
He goes to church each Sunday. His wife sings in the choir.
The kids graduated high school then took it even higher.

A simple man, a simple prayer, a heart that's racked with pain.
Sometimes Gods best blessings
Fall down just like rain.

The Kind of Nurse that You Could Be

Walking up and down the hallways
doing just what you do.
No one knows the reason
is just because you're you.

Though seldom is there ever.
Not a smile on your face.
No doubt there have been times.
Your smile felt out of place.

Still you rise above it.
You know somehow somewhere.
There is a hurting soul.
That needs you then and there.

Hours are long and nights are short.
You seem to pay no mind.
This is the job the life you chose.
It's not a daily grind.

It's not about your status
or about the money earned.
But for the sick and injured
you've always been concerned.

Somewhere in your mind's eye
you could somehow see.
With the heart that beats in you
the kind of nurse that you could be.

Two Sisters

To Angela and Heather
Best Friends Tribute

I've seen love of lovers.
Blossom and then grow.
But love between two sisters.
Only sisters know.

Though born of different mothers
sisters just the same.
Sharing almost everything.
Yet with a different name.

Watching from a distance
your special love is clear.
It's seen in spite of boundaries.
It lives in spite of fear.

For though fear at times exists
it's fear not of one another.
The only fear you know
is when you fear one for the other.

When things don't seem to go right
one of you gets bad news.
It's not long thereafter.
You both have the blues.

How it is will always be
as it's been right from the start.
Though you did not know at birth
you're connected at the heart.

All the hopes and dreams you have.
The many things you share.
Each is just another way.
You two show you care

Give It All To Him

Times when life seems brutal
things get too demanding.
There's nowhere to turn
to find some understanding.
Your heart is filled with fear.
Nights are lonely and so cold.
Things you used to enjoy.
Have suddenly all grown old.

Days when there's no escaping
the troubles on your mind.
I know a place on earth to go.
For the peace you hope to find.
It seems a friend cannot be found
when you most need them.
When you've taken all you're able.
Then give it all to Him.

When betrayed by others.
A loved one has turned away.
It seems to you it's over.
There's nothing left to say.
A loved one left before you.
They wait on the heavenly shore.
Your spirit feels so broken.
You can't take anymore.

The doctor's office called you.
They found some more bad news.
Nothing you can seem to do.
Helps you shake your blues.
When all the days that lie ahead
started looking cold and grim.
The place to find some solace
is in giving it all to Him.

Grace

So many times things come up I don't know what to say.
On those days I turn to God fall on my knees and pray.

When it comes to babies little children and such.
It affects us deeply because we love them all so much.

It can be so frightening when it happens to our own.
No matter if they're very young or even if they're grown.

But God knows everything that stands up in our way.
And wants us to turn to Him fall on our knees and pray.

To take what's on our hearts. Place it before Gods face.
And ask Him for a miracle. And ask Him for His Grace.

For it was God that made us and granted us our lives.
To teach us to have faith in Him until our miracle arrives.

So God we stand before you praying as if one.
Knowing only by Your grace can Your will be done.

So touch us with Your healing God give us strength today.
As we turn our faith to You fall on our knees and pray.

The Potter

Convinced you'll never make it.
You hurt so through and through.
No doubt if your heart remains.
It's broke clear in two.
At night when you lay down to sleep
you secretly whisper a prayer.
That tomorrow when the sun comes up
you won't still be there.

That there is somehow some relief
while in your dreams so deep.
That God in all His mercy
will call you while you sleep.
Then waking still just to find
that no one heard you pray.
Digging deep within yourself
you face yet another day.

God has seen you hurting.
When you hurt He hurts too.
Hang on a little longer
because He's not done with you.
Soon your sun will start to shine.
It's just a little while.
When your cleansing tears are gone
you will find your smile.

When the potter makes His masterpiece
it must first be tried by fire.
Only then it can be used
to meet the Kings desire.
To fill it with His treasures
with gifts sent from above.
But first it must be empty.
To make room for Gods love.

Written In Red

At first when you see it. It's seen a better day.
It looks a lot like something. That should be thrown away.

There were pages missing some just falling out.
It's fought a long hard battle down a lonely road of doubt.

Always on the table at night right by his bed.
He said the very best part. Were the words written in red.

He's carried it in two wars. He had it most his life
He got it on the very day. He married his first wife.

Back then it was a beauty. It's cover black with gold.
Just like him the many miles. Has made it look that old.

There was writing on its pages where he would make a note.
Only he and Jesus knew just what he wrote.

His old beat up bible has been a good friend.
He planned to take it with him when he met his end.

When he lay at his viewing his casket open wide.
There lay that old bible. Right there by his side.

With a single torn out page that lay there by his head.
The only thing he'd underlined. Were
the words written in red.

For Granted

A woman sits next to a grave
her eyes on its headstone.
She whispers mom I'm sorry.
Why'd you leave me all alone?
Times I took you for granted.
I didn't mean to be that way.
I never really thought.
That you would leave someday.

I know somehow I will survive.
Right now it's a living hell.
I guess I never understood.
How I got by so well.
Now I see it clearly.
As heavens gates bust open wide.
You gave everything you had
when I had you by my side.

You gave me what I wanted
and filled my every need.
I find it overwhelming.
As it's my turn now to lead.
What am I to do now?
What is there that I must know?
To keep mine from making these mistakes
as they continue now to grow.

Mom I hope that you can hear me.
No more tears fall from your eyes.
I hope you find rest in heaven.
And that you hear no more lies.
And as I start getting older
when I don't know what to do.
May I find the strength I need
mom, to be like you.

Empty Tomb

On the day that Jesus died.
When he drew His last
breath. He went into
the depths of hell.
And He defeated death.
He built a road to heaven.
Not made of dirt or mud.
The road He made to heaven is covered with His blood.
He could have called ten thousand angels. But He chose
to make His stand .He took the key to the gates of hell.
Right from the devils
Hand .He stood against
the demons. And He
withstood the fire.
Accomplishing His Fathers
wish. Fulfilling His desire.
In three days He rose again.
All of this for you and me.
I once was lost but now
am found. Was blind
but now I see . So
when troubles all
surround you. All you
feel is gloom. Remember
He is risen. The proof an
empty tomb.

He Holds Tomorrow

There are times in life. Only few know so well.
Circumstances beyond control life becomes a living hell.

Adversity abounds. Life simply rearranges.
We cling to what is dear accepting of life's changes.

Our past becomes our happy place. The future is unknown.
We draw from our memories. All the love we've shown.

Taking care of loved ones meeting their every need.
Standing right beside them no matter word or deed.

Hoping against hope things will turn around.
Praying every moment sometimes without a sound.

Feeling so alone encouragement gets spoken.
Still you can't deny. The fact your heart is broken.

From one day to another as you take life in stride.
Trying to hide the hopelessness that you feel inside.

Sitting quietly in your room no one hears your sighs.
But you have the promise. God hears His Children's cries.

No way to know the future. Be it happiness or sorrow.
May it bring some comfort to know He holds tomorrow.

Parables and Poetry

When Jesus talked in parables
right from the very start.
He did so to separate
those with a hardened heart.

For it is God that reveals
the message that's been sent.
And only in a fertile heart
can one know what it meant.

Poetry and parables
though not quite the same.
Every one may read them
they call not every name.

Some look without seeing.
Some hear not a word.
Their like a man trying to fly
without wings like a bird.

Parables and poetry
like writing in the sand.
A message etched into the heart.
Of those that understand.

For it is God that reveals
the message that's been sent.
And only in a fertile heart
can one know what it meant.

The Sparrow

When times of trouble find you
your heart is filled with fear.
Turn to Him inside you
for He is always near.

The road ahead is frightful
you don't know what to do.
Cast your eyes on Jesus
His eyes are on you..

Like the sparrow in the sky
He knows when they fall.
He gave not His life for sparrows
you mean more to Him than all.

You struggle with uncertainty
your mind is filled with doubt.
The strength you need will come
from the inside out.

When you find that what you have
you need a little more.
In your heart you hold the key
to open heaven's door.

Faith is as a mustard seed
it's tiny from the start.
Plant it and then watch it grow
it will flourish in your heart.

The road ahead is frightful
you don't know what to do.
Cast your eyes on Jesus
His eyes are on you..

Judgment over me.

Would you trade some sunshine
for just a little rain?
Give up a moments pleasure
to ease a strangers pain?

Can you heal a leper?
Turn water into wine?
Would you sacrifice your life
to save a life like mine?

Can you walk on water?
Make a blind man see?
Then don't think for a moment
you stand in judgment over me.

I've been told and I believe.
only God can judge.
You have an opinion.
and I don't hold a grudge.

Do you lead your brother?
By the life you live?
Have you cast out demons?
Have you power to forgive?

Have you served one that serves you?
Do you humbly wash their feet?
Do you give thanks to God above?
Before you break bread to eat?

Have you called out in a storm?
And calmed a raging sea?
Then don't think for a minute
you stand in judgment over me.

Give It All To Me

I saw a man on a bench we were sitting in a park.
We spent the whole day talking til long after dark.

It started with a question He asked what do you see.
I looked at him and almost cried. He said give it all to me.

I told him of my childhood like water on the sands.
And that's when I noticed the holes in both his hands.

Then I told him of my youth the trouble I'd been in.
When I glanced up at him He gave a knowing grin.

I looked deep into his eyes. Not understanding yet.
He said son this ain't the first time that you and I have met.

I saw you in your mother's womb I've been here all your days.
I know everything about you I've loved you for always

I've seen every tear you cried, I've heard the prayers you prayed.
Times when you pushed me away, I didn't leave I stayed.

I was the reason more than once. That you got your heart broke.
Times that you could not hear. The words to you I spoke.

The times I saw you suffer. I helped you make it through.
Because everything you've endured. I have suffered too.

You've yet so very much to learn. But one thing you must see.
Good bad or indifferent. Give it all to me.

Through my tears I bowed my head. My eyes were on the street.
Before He turned to walk away I saw holes in both His feet.

Gone before I knew it my life is now all changed.
It seems my whole outlook is completely rearranged.

Every injury I've suffered. I've forgiven all of them.
If you ask me how I did it. I gave it all to Him.

Jesus Had Been Here.

I was aware in a dream I was a beggar in the street.
My legs bent and badly broken I would beg for food to eat.
I watched them from a distance. I crawled slowly through the sand.
Suddenly there was silence. As He bent down and took my hand.

"Be thee whole!" Are the words He said. I felt His power enter me.
I began to rise and walk. He said "God had mercy on thee."
Then I found myself in a cave. In the rocks just off the sea.
Tormented by many demons. Then He came and rescued me.

I saw me filled with leprosy. I made my way through the crowd.
When I reached out and touched Him. He turned and cried out loud.
"Who is the one that touched Me? I felt virtue leave my soul."
He found me scared and trembling. "He said your faith has made thee whole."

Suddenly my eyes went dark. I dreamed I had gone blind.
When I heard Him speak to me. He was loving and so kind.
I felt His fingers touch my eyes. He forgave me all my sin.
He told me "go and witness." And tell my story to all men.

The last part of the dream I had. Left me at such a loss.
I was a thief that hung by Him. As He hung there on that cross.
I called out "He's done nothing." I begged them to let Him be.
I watched His mother as she wept. But they could not set Him free.

He told me with His dying breath. Through His suffering I heard Him say.
"You will be at my Father's side. With Me in heaven on this day."
When I awoke I wasn't shaking. I somehow knew no fear.
My spirit was my witness. That Jesus had been here.

Gravy Train

They met on the internet. The relationship just flourished.
First time they met in person. She knew he was malnourished.

She took him home and fed him. Fried chicken and tators too.
Covered in homemade gravy. And before the meal was through.

He vowed to stay forever. She said he's crazy as a bat.
He said he'd never leave her. If she can cook like that!

Next morning he had ham and eggs. With a side of some french toast.
The look she saw in his eyes. Said I love you the most.

When the meal was over. He sat her on his lap.
He promised her a diamond ring.When he woke up from his nap.

Twenty five years later. He still eats like a horse.
When he asks for homemade gravy. She smiles and says of course.

He says he loves her meatloaf. Her pork chops are the best.
When she fries up some chicken. He lets her have the breast.

She makes awesome burgers. When she throws in some fries.
It gives her the shivers. To see the love light in his eyes.

They'll always be together. Cause he's crazy as a bat.
He will never leave her. Cause she can cook like that!

The Only One I Missed!

We met on a winter night.
Through the internet.
I think she is beautiful.
Though I haven't seen her yet.
We typed away the hours.
We chatted all night long.
I even copied and pasted.
The words of her favorite song.
I loved her from the moment.
I saw (Thanks for the add).
I sent an anniversary card.
To her mom and dad.
I tried my best I really did.
She just couldn't love me back.
She said we were like oil and water.
It was written in white and black.
So then I met her sister.
Her favorite cousin and her nieces.
Before the year was over.
I loved that family to pieces.
Sometimes I think about her.
And about her family.
And wonder why they hate me.
Filled with negativity.
Don't get me wrong I don't regret.
All the ones I kissed.
I just can't stop thinking about.
The only one I missed.

The Cleaner

He's needin him some lovin.
He knows how to make her hot.
He puts on an apron.
And starts struttin what he's got.
He plugs in the vacuum.
And vacuums up the floor.
She'll be so surprised
When she walks in the door.

He polishes the furniture
He washes every dish.
He knows she won't say no.
When he tells her his wish.
Then he grabs the laundry.
And starts another load.
Grads what's in the dryer.
And sits long enough to fold.

Grabs a bag of trash.
Then hauls it all outside.
Thinkin bout later on.
About a midnight ride.
The house is nearly spotless.
Tonight he'll see no wrath.
There's enough time left.
For him to take a bath.

He's soaking in some bubbles.
When he hears her hit the door.
He hollers out be careful.
I just mopped the floor.
A little later on he knows.
Her passion is hotwired.
But he says not tonight.
I'm sorry I'm too tired.

Desire

You see her from across the room.
There's desire in your eyes.
You strain your neck trying to see.
If you can see her thighs.

You move a little closer.
You're trying not to make a scene.
You find an extra plate.
You make sure it's clean.

Your eyes are almost frantic.
They wont give it a rest.
They find what you are looking for.
You're staring at her breast.

You glance around one more time.
It's time to make your play.
You step boldly forward.
Then turn around and say.

Hey! Anybody gonna eat these
last couple pieces of chicken?

Full Grown Girl

I got a friend his name is Tom. He likes his women thin.
He don't understand at all. I like mine built for men.

Someone when I'm holding them. They can hold me back.
Someone that can take it. When I go on attack.

Someone soft and tender. Not built like a stick.
Someone warm and caring. I like my women thick.

He likes his not too tall. Shaped just like a pole.
I want one that can give me. Some old time rock and roll.

Someone that likes her gravy. Made like I like mine.
If she can fry up bacon. We'll get along just fine.

I love the pretty smelling hair. I adore some pretty eyes.
But I don't want a kiddie meal. Make mine super size.

I want a little wiggle. Every time she walks.
Tom he likes the arbie type. And don't care if she talks.

Me. I want to feel her. When she climbs into bed.
I wanna know she's really there. And not just in my head.

I couldn't make him understand. We agreed to disagree.
He can have his itty bitty. It's a full grown girl for me.

Digging all of you.

I know this may sound silly
And you may think I'm a nut.
But I've been having dreams.
About my hands on your butt.
I'm not trying to offend you
So please don't think me crass
Its just that my mind wandered
Then landed on your ass.

I picture us just standing
In a lovers warm embrace.
My hand finds your butt cheek
And that look on your face.
I don't know how it happened
How my mind wandered south.
Just yesterday I was thinking.
About your face and mouth.

The day before my imagination
Had my fingers in your hair.
So I guess it's only natural.
My mind would end up there.
Tonight as I close my eyes.
And try to get some rest.
I'm going to practice self control
So I don't think about your breast.

So I am going to focus.
On whispering in your ear.
To see if that won't help me.
Get my mind of your rear.
So don't think me perverted.
By these crazy things I do.
It's just my way of saying.
That I am digging all of you.

Holiday Romance!

I knew today was special.
As I walked into the store.
Most were here for groceries.
But I was here for more.

I couldn't help but notice.
She stood out from all the rest.
I felt completely unashamed.
I reached out to touch her breast.

I gently picked her up.
And held her in my arms.
Just one more of many.
That has fallen for her charms.

She was the one I searched for.
How could this be wrong?
It seemed that I've been wanting her.
For oh so very long.

I gently traced my fingertips.
Up her legs onto her thighs.
We hid behind the produce.
To avoid the prying eyes.

I thought I heard her whisper.
As she called my name out more.
Then they took my turkey.
And threw me out of the store.

Next morning in the paper.
I read in written word.
Local man goes to jail.
For trying to stuff a bird.

Cereal Killer

The story of his life.
A made for TV thriller.
Title in blood red.
Life of a cereal killer.
He don't want no fried eggs.
Or peanut butter toast.
He killed a box of grape nuts once!
But he don't like to boast.

He has Wheaties for his breakfast.
Cheerios for his lunch.
For a mid day snack.
He likes Captain Crunch.
He don't want a T-bone.
He don't want French silk.
Corn flakes and some sugar.
In a bowl of milk.

Along about suppertime.
As he hides from the cops.
Sitting in the shadows.
Munching sugar pops.
He don't mean to scare you.
Sometimes he behaves.
Even when it's boo berry.
Or count chocula that he craves.

He's no threat to society.
At a table or a booth.
He's just a cereal killer.
With a really bad sweet tooth.
From early dawn til after dusk.
He's never gonna stop.
You hear him in his kitchen.
Going snap crackle and pop!

Call Out My Name.

I am the last thing that you think of.
When you lay down at night.
You don't walk you run to me.
When you wake to mornings light.

You love the very taste of me.
When you feel me in your mouth.
You love my warmth inside you.
And the way it travels south.

When I'm gone you long to have me.
A craving you can't explain.
You want me in your body.
When you have me on your brain.

You know when I am nearby.
By your sense of smell.
One day goes by without me.
Feels like a living hell.

You need me more than want me.
But you want me just the same.
While you wait impatiently.
You call out my name.

Signed: Coffee

Well-Mart

So you say you've seen it all?
I'll bet I can show you more.
Take a little ride with me.
Have a seat just inside the door.
See that lady over there?
Hanging out of her pants?
Or the guy talking to himself?
Have you listened to his rants?

Check out the one on her way out.
She's wearing her pajamas.
From the looks of the holes in them.
They used to be her gramma's.
There's a guy over there.
He's only got one sneaker.
He's standing there next to the girl.
That looks just like a tweeker.

I know that it's not nice to judge.
People do have rights.
I'm not passing judgment.
We're just checking out the sights.
Check out the gangsta over there.
His pants around his knees.
Oops he's not a gangsta.
He's one of the employees.

I see you're getting tired.
You need a therapists touch.
I guess we stayed a bit too long.
And now you've seen too much.
Just stand here for a minute.
And hold on to this cart.
I hope you enjoyed your visit.
Thank for shopping at Well Mart.

Rise Again

Many many years ago.
God looked years ahead.
He saw the longing in you.
And this is what He said.
"Knock and the door will be opened.
Seek and you shall find.
Come unto me those who weep.
And rest your weary mind."

Then He sent those that heard Him.
To go find the ones in need.
To share with them the good news.
And plant in them this seed.
No longer must you live in doubt.
During times you cannot cope.
Jesus Christ is risen.
And lives to bring you hope.

So cast on Him your troubles.
And the shadows of the night.
Turn your face to heaven.
And look into the light.
For nothing can defeat you.
As you dare to make your stand.
When angels go before you.
And you hold heavens hand.

Be assured times will come.
You don't where to start.
At times like this you hear Him.
By listening to your heart.
And when troubles find you.
And heartache should begin.
Like Jesus did so long ago.
You must learn to rise again.

Suddenly

When a loved one leaves us suddenly.
Our heart is so easily broken.
Flooded with their memory.
And words that went unspoken.

The secret to finding comfort.
Is in knowing what you feel.
They too have known all along.
The bond you had was real.

Your love for one another.
Is written in the skies.
The words you think you didn't say.
You said with your eyes.

Still your heart keeps aching.
Tears fall down your face.
You can't begin to imagine.
Who will take their place.

The fact is though they are gone.
Yet they still are near.
For you never really lose the one.
That you hold so dear.

They live and breath inside you.
It's how they show they care.
Bringing comfort to you.
With each memory you share.

So though your heart is troubled.
And your eyes are filled with tears.
Remember they are with you now.
And will be all your years.

Unbroken

No less than amazing, bruised but never broken.
Crying out within us, though words are never spoken.

Helping us to rise again un-accepting of defeat.
Even when we stand alone, making us complete.

Teaching us compassion, and empathy for others.
Causing us to reach out to our sisters and our brothers.

Giving us such visions, as making the world a better place.
Filling us with courage for the obstacles we will face.

Giving us the freedom to dream when all else fails.
Silently and invisibly, blowing wind into our sails.

It never seeks permission to rise up from within.
And each time that we lose our way, it rises up again.

It warns of impending danger to our left or to our right.
It stops our knees from shaking, if we should choose to fight.

And should we decide the thing to do is turn and run away.
It offers us encouragement, to live and fight another day.

It brings a smile to the lips of each person when they hear it.
For the thing that I am speaking of, is the human spirit.

The Longing: A Mothers Love

Six years seems like a thousand. Without you by my side.
You're always in my heart and mind. My arms stay open wide.

Emotions overtake me. As I long to find a way.
To let you know I love you. There's so much I want to say.

Just over fifteen years ago. I felt so all alone.
Then I laid eyes on Laura. A baby girl of my own.

We weathered many storms. Rain and wind unfurled.
Darling please remember. You were and are my world.

A day does not pass by me I don't look up at the skies.
And get lost in the memory. Of the love in your blue eyes.

It wasn't too long after that. My world was filled with joy,
You called him your brother. My bouncing baby boy.

Though becoming a young man. And time can take a toll.
Eric please believe me. When I say you are my soul.

No doubt you are growing fast. The whole world waits to see.
The rising star within you. And the man you'll someday be.

I cling daily to the hope. Missing you both will someday end.
When we can hold each other close.
And let our heartaches mend.

If you should ever wonder. As you wish upon a star.
My love will be forever. Right there where you are.

And should you ever need me. Though a thousand miles apart.
Close your eyes and think of me. Your always in my heart.

Let Her Go.

Tenderly he runs his hand.
Across her wrinkled brow.
Whispers it will be ok.
He knows it won't somehow.
Fifty years they've been together.
He knows he doesn't know.
If he can face life without her.
He don't want to let her go.

Sitting by her bedside.
He'd give her his last breath.
He always thought he'd be first.
When it came to death.
Now sitting here just watching.
As nature take it's place.
He thinks it aint right.
As tears roll down his face.

Reaching out once again.
He takes her by the hand.
Thinks about the things in life.
He may never understand.
Kissing her on the cheek.
He say's I want you to know.
If it were all up to me.
I'd never let you go.

But life is one big mystery.
We've never been apart.
Thinking about it sitting here.
All but breaks my heart.
Somewhere while he talked to her.
He didn't even know.
She headed on to heaven.
And he just let her go.

"My Only One"

He watched from the window. As she worked in the yard.
His lips formed to a smile. She's always worked so hard.

It seemed not so long ago. She was out there planting seeds.
But days like years move forward. Now she's out there pulling weeds.

He longs to go out to her. And help her with her chores.
But those days are far behind him. For now he walks through doors.

He hears her as she comes back in. From her day out in the sun.
She picks up his picture. And says "Hows my only one?"

He recalls when it happened. The day her true love died.
He lost control in the blinding snow. Trying to get here by her side.

There was talk among her family. That she would lose her mind.
And that's when he decided. That he would stay behind.

Her friends don't come around no more. They say she isn't right.
She walks through their tiny home. And talks to him at night.

Then she sits and holds his picture. And stares out at the moon.
Vowing her undying love. They will be together soon.

He longs to kiss and hold her. He knows she knows he's there.
He wants to reach out to her. But he knows that he don't dare.

So the man whose picture she clings to. The man that has her heart.
Are forever now together. But for now still far apart.

He stands quiet across the room. As she makes her way to bed.
Then whispers to her darling. It's time to rest your pretty head.

It seems almost unfair to me. How two that loved the most.
Could be stuck here in this moment. A woman and a ghost.

One More Before I Go

Back when we were kids
Too young to really know.
If there were treats available.
I'd have one before I go.
I'd watch out the car window.
Til we went around the bend.
I saved all your letters.
With the love that you would send.

As we got a little older.
We hugged when I arrived.
Talk and joke and wonder.
How we both survived.
When it came time to leave.
With more love than we could show.
As we hugged each other.
I'd say one more before I go.

The miles in between us.
Made visits few and far between.
Had it not been for photographs.
We never would have seen.
That we kept getting older.
Our hair was turning gray.
Had it not been for letters.
We'd had nothing much too say.

But when I heard the news.
I came as fast as I could.
You knew I would take your place.
If only that I could.
But standing by your death bed.
You smiled. And I said I know.
As we hugged each other.
You whispered One more before I go.

GOING HOME.

As I think about the future. And all the things I left behind.
Remembering what I wished I'd done. Almost blows my mind.

I wish as a young man. When trouble came my way.
That I had the answers. That I now have today.

I wish as I got older. That I hadn't been afraid.
When I was with children. I had joined in while they played.

But now those days are past me. My end is now at hand.
I used to walk for miles. Now I can barely stand.

So to all or those I've loved. And that loved me in return.
Keep watch of where you're going. As well as bridges that you burn.

Today is what you're given. Yesterday now is past.
Tomorrow is not promised. So enjoy them while they last.

Help someone that needs it. As you travel on your way.
I'll see you on the other side. On some sweet sunny day.

Angels Wing.

Stepping through a curtain. Into heaven from earth below.
I thought I must have died. And I didn't even know.

I looked all around me. Everything was white.
It looked like everything that moved. Was made out of light.

First I saw my grandma. She was walking with my dad.
My heart was overjoyed. I thought heaven aint so bad.

I saw all the friends I knew. In my life before.
Then I saw John come running. He don't need that chair no more!

They sky was blue the ground was gold. No sign of any rain.
I noticed when I took a step. I no longer was in pain.

There were angels singing. Praises to the lord.
There were children playing. Not one of them was bored.

Then a great light shined on me. It was Jesus, Gods own Son.
He said that I must come back. My work was not yet done.

They all smiled at me and waved. I turned to find a stream.
When I awoke I was at home. It must have been a dream.

As I sat and pondered. I remembered everything.
Then I saw on my sill. A feather from an angels wing.

Dearly Beloved

The crowd all whispers quietly. Gathered to show respect.
Flowers around the coffin. Not a thing did they neglect.

At that very same moment. Heaven was shining bright.
Not everyone was invited. To the party here tonight.

The preacher prays a solemn prayer. On earth down here below.
While angels all in heaven. Get ready for the show.

People quietly dry their eyes. As tears roll down their face.
While all the saints in heaven. All gather in one place.

Someone sings amazing grace. While family members weep.
While above a joyous celebration. A tradition they must keep.

The preacher makes an alter call. Then bows his head to pray.
And prays for all those left behind. And strength for the next day.

But in heaven the place is rocking. St Peter and the angels sing.
Harps they all are playing. The church bells start to ring.

There's a party at the pearly gates. The dancing's already started.
Only those that don't understand. Feel down and brokenhearted.

All of heaven celebrates. The arrival of a soul.
No longer stuck down here on earth. Now
God can make them whole.

If you've traveled with me this far as we have been stepping form the shadows. Maybe this is a good place to rest for just a moment and talk. At this very moment it occurs to me that instead of having seven or eight categories for my poems. I easily could have knocked it down to three and changed its name to The Good, Bad and the Ugly.

The (Good) being the poems about the joys in life. About love and walking on the clouds or dancing in the rain. The (Bad) Quite possibly be every poem I thought to be funny or cute when it was written. And the (Ugly) is what waits for us beyond this page.

Because we all know that life is not always about dreams coming true and broken hearts healing. It's not always about clear lines being drawn in the sand and giving us directions. There are things in life we struggle to understand. Something we may never be able to do if those things remain hidden. In the shadows if you will.

Things like abuse, addiction, depression and many more. It was suggested to me that I include some of these poems mostly that when written were requested by people who found themselves in the midst of these very things. If not them it was someone close to them. And therefore if you choose to read past this page. I would like to challenge you just a little bit farther. As you read the lines of the next few pages someone you know may very well come to mind. It may even be you. But I ask as that other person crosses your mind that you make a note of it and some time very soon share that poem with them. It's possibly them it was written for. Together we can invite them to Step from the Shadows with us.

Edwin C Hofert

Hide Out In The Open.

You've seen him there so often.
You barely notice anymore.
He never says a single word.
He just stares down at the floor.

There's a thousand more just like him.
It doesn't matter where you go.
A junkie in a corner.
That's praying you won't know.

They've given up on themselves.
And on hopin. Their just copin.
Too strung out to run away.
And so they hide out in the open.

He feels almost invisible.
To those that pass on by.
They can't see his hopes and dreams.
They can't hear his hearts cry.

He's convinced nobody notices.
None sees him standing there.
No one ever asks his name.
There's no reason they should care.

No clue what he's been through.
He's taken life's hard licks.
Now he hides out in the open.
Waiting for just one more fix.

Depressions Confessions

A storm is brewing in your heart.
You've learned to read the signs.
It's like trying to color.
But you can't see the lines.
The skies within are turning gray.
The storms about to begin.
You wish that you could stop it.
The depressions moving in.

The joy so often you express.
Has suddenly grown quiet.
You tell them all that you're okay.
So they're not bothered by it.
You've been here so many times.
You can't take this anymore.
Each time it comes over you.
It's worse than the time before.

You do you best to hide it.
But no matter how one tries.
There's a window to your soul.
That God placed in your eyes.
You know that you'll make it.
Though you're uncertain how.
You tell yourself you need some help.
But you don't need it now.

A lifetimes takes a minute.
Think of the choice your choosing.
Each time you have an episode.
Think of all your losing.
You shouldn't have to live like this.
You've heard yourself say.
Listen to yourself for once.
Go get some help today.

Aaron

So you don't believe in miracles?
I know one here on earth.
He's been our little miracle.
Since the day of his birth.
Oh we had some problems.
Our hearts were filled with fear.
He was quite the fighter.
That much is still clear.

There's days that it aint easy.
Some things don't go as planned.
The farthest thing from our minds.
Was being unable to walk or stand.
But when you see him in action.
I may never know just why.
What keeps that chair on the ground?
I swear he could make it fly.

He zips around the corners.
Like they're no there at all!.
And that's not even half of it!
You should see him hit a ball!
He's like a secret agent man.
Rolling around the bases.
When he gets a little older.
I'll bet he'll win some races.

Trophies all around his room
For things that he has won.
There's no way of knowing.
How much he's already done.
He came in this world fighting.
And in ways he's fighting still.
We sure love our Aaron.
And I know we always will.

Sleeping With The Enemy

She sits alone and contemplates. She's living in such fear.
Wondering what she forgot this time.
She knows he'll soon be here.

Sometimes the way he looks at her. She fears it is her fate.
To be stuck here forever. With a man so full of hate.

He seems kind and charming. When others are around.
Sometimes she thinks her relief. Will
be when she's in the ground.

She has just vague memories. Of the dreams that she once had.
She wonders what she did. That things turned out so bad.

Sometimes when he's not at home. She prays to God above.

She asks Him to change things. All she wanted was his love.

She loves him but don't like him. Some days she's just not sure.
That her body mind and soul. Can learn to endure.

The abuse he dishes out to her. When he starts to curse.
It's happening more often. And it keeps getting worse.

She wonders does God hear her? Whenever that she prays.
She doesn't know what to do. That's one reason that she stays.

She knows that she's strong. But she can't take no more.
Suddenly her fear returns.
His key is in the door.

The climb

A beauty by any standard.
A heart as pure as gold.
Any man on earth would be.
Proud to have her to hold.
But sometimes our eyes deceive us.
It was not as it seemed to be.
What everybody else believed.
Was not what she could see.

Abused from just a child.
Many secrets hidden there.
She could not imagine.
There's one that just might care.
Still she does her very best.
But alone at night she cries.
Not knowing that the one she loved.
Filled her heart with lies.

Each time that they touched her.
When they told her it was love.
And that there was no such thing.
As a God above.
Then one night at a revival.
She heard words that had been spoken.
The truth went straight into her heart.
That was for so long broken.

It took some time to understand.
That life had done her wrong.
But her faith began to grow.
Her love of God grew strong.
Now the pain she used to bear.
Sits unnoticed on a shelf.
Seeing now what we always did.
She's learned to love herself.

My World That I Call Chase

I've heard them call him special.
You can bet to me that's true.
The heart in him beats with mine.
As one instead of two.
Special in the love he gets.
And in the special love he gives.
Yes you could say he's special.
And it's so special to be his.

I've heard them say he's challenged.
We meet challenges every day.
And we'll try again tomorrow.
Til there's no more in our way.
There may be moments now and then.
That are hard on his mom and him.
But never for one second.
Will I give up on them.

Such a kind a caring soul.
He's has come so very far.
He's gone beyond the doctors dreams.
He is such a shining star.
When I see the special smile.
On his very special face.
It makes my whole world special.
My world that I call Chase.

So if you think it's a challenge?
And you think that we should quit.
You're some kind of special.
Or else you don't know Britt.
Autism is another word.
For awesome in his way.
You bet that boy is special.
And I thank God every day.

The Battle Rages

I've been gone so very long.
Lost in missing you sorrow.
Those days now all but gone.
I'm coming home tomorrow....

Though the war still rages.
I know what I'm to do.
Put away my combat boots.
And come on home to you.

The new recruits are younger.
Much like I used to be.
I come home with the honors.
Of serving my country.

Though I know I'll miss the troops.
That stood right by my side.
Each of them all wish me well.
As I come home to my bride.

The battles that we fought and won.
We still haven't won the war.
I gave all I had to give.
I can't give any more.

My family awaits me.
I'm a hero in their eyes.
I can't bear to see another.
As a good man dies.

So I'm coming home to all of you.
The war I leave behind.
No longer in the battle.
Except for in my mind.

His Fix

He takes his tiny package.
He just bought down the street.
He wanted it so badly.
Now he just feels defeat.
He'll deal with his emotions.
In a little bit.
Right now he just needs his fix.
And so he takes a hit.

Soon he's where he wants to be.
Another time another place.
As his drug induced smile.
Spreads across his face.
Then as he gets ready.
For the next hit he will take.
He see's his reflection.
He knows the smile is fake.

The tears he's held within.
Begin finding their way out.
Somehow he had forgotten.
What life is all about.
Everything he every wanted.
The prayers he used to pray.
All the love he ever knew.
Were things he threw away.

Then he sees the picture.
The son he aint seen in weeks.
The light shining in his eyes.
His chubby little cheeks.
Emotions overwhelming him.
His heart and mind begin to mix.
Choosing between the right thing.
Or the hand that holds his fix.

Playground In My Mind

How you used to run around.
In every playground you could find.
As you used to laugh and play.
In your playground in my mind....

The games you used to love to play.
Pull me close then push away.
Telling me how much you cared.
Not meaning what you say.

The pleasure you got from my pain.
With your deceit and strife.
As you laughed and played.
In your playground in my life.

As you rallied all your troops.
So they told the same lies.
Begging me to came back.

As fake tears fell from your eyes.

The way you relished your success.
As you tore my world apart.
As you laughed and ran around.
In your playground in my heart.

With all the games behind me now.
I've found a way to heal.
And I found one that gives a damn.
For the way I feel.

Still the memory haunts me.
Every once in awhile.
Like every time I pray for you.
Or I see the devil smile.

It is my wish that you have enjoyed Stepping From The Shadows.
And that somewhere in these pages you found some inspiration.
It occurs to me that when it comes to giving. That with each poem I write I'm giving you a
very real part of me. And in return in the reading of them you are opening up and giving
to me in return. And so it goes a constant cycle of us inspiring one another.
I pray that on days when you are weary and discouraged this book finds its way once again into
your hands and that you can find at least in part what will get you through the moment.
Thank you from the bottom of my heart for taking time to read the poems I wrote for you.

Edwin C Hofert
The Heart Whisperer

e.hofert@yahoo.com

Printed in the United States
By Bookmasters